s k i e s

Alison Brackenbury was born in
Lincolnshire in 1953, from a long
line of skilled farm workers. For
the last forty years she has lived in
Gloucestershire, where her varied
jobs included twenty-three years
working with her husband as a
metal finisher. Her poems (written
in small gaps between work, child,
horses, addictions to music and
grassroots politics) have won an
Eric Gregory and a Cholmondeley
Award. Recently retired from her
day job, she has become increas-
ingly interested in performing her
poetry, usually by heart.

s k i e s

ALISON BRACKENBURY

CARCANET

First published in Great Britain in 2016 by
Carcanet Press Limited
Alliance House, 30 Cross Street,
Manchester, M2 7AQ
www.carcanet.co.uk

A CIP catalogue record for this book is
available from the British Library,
ISBN 9781784101800

The publisher acknowledges financial
assistance from Arts Council England.

Supported using public funding by
ARTS COUNCIL
ENGLAND

CONTENTS

skies

HONEYCOMB

It is too beautiful to eat.
Knife crumbles it from gold to dark.
Our keenest edge cannot stay sharp
while in our walls, which seemed so strong,
damp murmurs with the evening sleet.
I wonder if I live too long

but then I taste the honeycomb,
its waxen white upon my teeth,
its liquid sun which hides beneath.
Small deities, of wind or moon,
behold me. In my shabby room
I am a god. I lick the spoon.

Sex is like Criccieth. You thought it would be
a tumble of houses into a pure sea
and so it must have been, in eighteen-ten.
The ranks of boarding houses marched up then.
They linger, plastic curtains at their doors,
or, more oddly, blonde ungainly statues.
The traffic swills along the single street
and floods the ears, until our feet
turn down towards the only shop for chips,
to shuffling queues, until sun slips
behind the Castle, which must be, by luck,
one of the few a Welsh prince ever took.
Or in the café, smoked with fat, you wait.
Will dolphins strike the sea's skin? They do not.

And yet, a giant sun nobody has told
of long decline, beats the rough sea to gold.
The Castle rears up with its tattered flag,
hand laces hand, away from valleys' slag.
And through the night, the long sea's dolphined breath
whispers into your warm ear, *Criccieth.*

VESTA TILLEY

(music hall star and recruiter)

Little Vesta had a mother
whom she would rarely see,
off touring with her father.
The dancing dog made three.

Her tiny shoes showed patent shine,
her shirts, a schoolboy's grace.
Her perfect tailored trousers
made the old Queen hide her face.

Vesta would claim her act was 'clean',
unlike that Marie Lloyd,
bedraggled, following the van.
Rich, sober, well-employed,

rocked only by the sudden night
her father's life was done,
little Vesta married
the theatre owner's son.

They stormed the States. They knocked on doors
which flustered women ran
to open, so her husband beat
that dreadful Labour man.

Though he was so much younger,
a foolish boy with flowers,
he died in Monte Carlo.
In rich blue empty hours

silent, she poured out memoirs,
twelve siblings; pro at six;
her father, cabs, the roaring halls,
Fathead the dog's sweet tricks.

What swelled her ruined throat with pride?
Her dearest trousered stunt,
the night she sent three hundred boys
straight to the Western Front.

TOLD

Ask everything you want to!
You cannot stay long.
No one, now, will ever hear
your father's father's songs.

I heard both songs and stories
from my mother's father's war.
But forty years from guns,
he grew a joyful liar.

He had seen every truce,
the football in the mud,
stood, he said, a batman, ironing,
to the great guns' thud.

No one else spoke of the mules,
led where no rail could run,
of axles, bubbling under mud
where useless wheels spun.

So every story ended
as his wife set cups for three,
'Then the mule kicked the Major –
so we laughed and drank our tea.'
Then the mule kicked the Major.
So we laughed, and drank our tea.

MY GRANDMOTHER SAID

It was the First World War.
Her husband was away.
She knew fear, but also found
new freedom in the day.

On Thursdays, with the farmer's wife,
old basket in her lap,
by butter slabs, she rode to Brigg,
shawled, in the pony trap.

Oh how I envied her!
I whined to Brigg by bus,
for school, no pony's dancing knees,
first sun in elder bush.

She would have crossed the Ancholme,
seen the canal glint wide.
She could buy apples and white thread,
jog home, to new moon's rise.

'But I was frozen, to my bones,
all winter.' Was that all?
My grandfather took up the reins.
She settled in her shawl.

JANUARY

a poem for radio

Harsh, hateful month, yet morning's moon,
my silver penny, dear as dark,
floods ash buds black, as first cars fume.
For January brings work, work, work.
Have you heard the town foxes bark?
How screams as sharp as yours or mine,
hungry and raw as children, spark
our small rooms by the railway line?

Work ends. In hills' dusk I leave cars,
call my old horse. Mists wreathe and pass.
Our heated world already stars
daisies across the hoof-pocked grass.
The rescued mare, found fly-grazed, thin,
now trots with Christmas foal at heels.
My horse has tasted thirty springs.
All charge for stables, leave night's fields.

From January's dark and freezing rain
I reach my kitchen's warm cocoon.
I dream of my grandmother's pudding,
hot steamed sponge sliding from the spoon
with dripping amber, her plum jam,
lost summer caught in red jars' rank.
She fed her neighbour's hungry son,
I find tinned beans for a food bank.

Are you in your warm kitchen now?
Keep off the killing New Year's dark
which has drunk some we love, but how
in mud, in rooms, we make our mark.
Peel the potatoes. Stir the spoon.
I hope, before lit days, and many,
you meet a January moon.
How will you spend your silver penny?

8 A.M.

I am cycling, in a sensible, bright coat.
A girl comes pedalling quickly by, loose shawls
skidding from shoulders, hitched skirt, silver pumps.
I was that girl. O may she ride her falls.

SO

This is the trouble with spring. The snow comes down,
and it is all gone, under drift, dune, powder,
cats must be tunnelled for, dogs retrieved,
while milk is a dream, down the next street.

The cars stall on the hill.
Their wheels spin, then scream. The migrant jay
flashes for food. Blue is the wing
of the truant sky, soared Swiss, and pitiless.

How sudden the thaw is. Out of its burrow
the lawn creeps, tired but safe. The streets run smooth once more.
The cold no longer aches. At the end of a war,
your life limps home. And you are not sure that you want it.

And the rain stopped. And the sky spun
past the hills' flush of winter corn.
The mare strode out as though still young.

You walked. I almost said, last year
I saw a hare run with her young
just past the broken wall, just here.

Two flew in circles. First, one rose
upon its great back legs. It boxed
at air. The second flinched, then rose.

England has blackbirds, mice. To find
these strong black shapes makes the heart race
as barley under icy wind.

Boxing is courtship, failed. One broke,
tore past us to the rough safe hedge.
She crossed the sun. Her colours woke,

ears black, back russet, earth new-laid.
Her legs stretched straight. The late showers made
bright water fly from every blade.

PROLOGUE

I need five hundred serious words. But still
the pure black kitten in an upstairs window
chases its tail, in ecstasy and boredom.
I cannot start till it falls off the sill.

HALF-FLEDGED

The silks lay fanned out in the sewing box.
You fingered red. It trembled first as rose,
smouldered back to crimson's blackest close.
What could you make of this? Materials mock
your clumsy hand. Though you could hem a seam
you chose the dullest template, spent a day
on half a daisy; packed the box away.

But here it is. The baby greenfinch flies
out of the lane's dust, with an olive sheen
blooming his back, each tender shade between
to lemon wing-bars, safe from farm-cats' eyes.
For half a mile it bobs below the showers,
flits to a tree; embroiders elderflowers.

AT THE BUS STOP

Then I saw a woman
come slowly down the road,
a child's jumper folded
on her arm.

She wore a pale mac
and the thinnest of black stockings,
stepped stiffly, as if air
might do her harm.

The jumper was light green,
badged for the school
she reached so slowly. Small trees
chattered into leaf.

Though, maybe, she forgot,
then fetched his uniform,
she seemed a tiny part:
one whole and perfect grief.

What am I good at? Useless things.
Listening to strangers on slow Scottish trains.
Did you know they had square sausages?
Standing on one leg – not yoga; muddy years of Wellingtons.
And peeling parsnips. Cooking grand Christmas dinner,
amongst dried cranberries, asparagus,
my daughter passed the knife, then was surprised
my awkward hands whipped smoothly down each root,
flicked pale gold slivers, thin, to save the flesh
that frost and soil had left as sweet as nuts,
which you may understand. And I remember
in tea's cold deeps, although the saucepans steamed,
caught in a creaking visit once, I said,
(mouth full) 'These are good parsnips! Did you grow them?'
'Yes', said my father, shrunk to eighty years,
nodded with dignity, like his tall father.
We were not good with words. Each time my hand
slips down, as sharp as winter, and casts off
a pale coat, I am grateful, still, to parsnips.

PAINTED BIRD, FOUND IN A ROMAN GRAVE

'They left this cockerel by the head
so Mercury could reach the dead.
The cockerel is his messenger.'
I thought after the expert spoke
they set it so, as in a bed,
the child would see it when he woke.

THREE POEMS FROM STEEP

(I) Letter, 1917

I had one dream in France,
curled up before the fight.
I fell past the bugles,
stray blackbirds, stabs of light,
landed by our table.
Though you clasped Baba, smiled to me,
I was a sort of visitor, and
I could not stay for tea.

(II) No 2, Yewtree Cottages

This was your garden. And the grass is long.
Rough as a child's hair. The wind gusts strong.
Only the half-pruned hazels in the hedge
shelter the new stone pigs, by the path's edge,

broad rue bush, grey with buds, high fat for birds
you might have bought, if men paid more for words.
Stray vegetables, too few to meet your needs,
break old black garden soil, part-raked for seeds.

Is nothing left? A book, a garden tool?
Does the cramped house recall you, kind or cruel?
The March light, like a soldier's body, thinned,
sweeps us down your cracked path, out with the wind.

(III) Visitor

But while I wait by that low door
where he would duck, though rarely shout
I sense harsh pressure thrust me back,
someone in pain, who must walk out.

PLAYGROUND

Children, you lined up for your game;
one tall boy called, 'Sheep, sheep, come home.
The wolf has gone to Derbyshire.
He won't come back for seven years.'
You raced across the wind-blurred ground.
But he was wolf. He plunged, he pounced.
Each child, when he clutched coat or cuff,
straight-haired, scuff-toed, became the wolf.

Are you a wolf, grey, slender? Yet
as, elegantly, you stroll through
the café's buzz, the city's dome,
what is it you do not forget?
How even then they lied to you?
Still they sing out, 'Sheep, sheep, come home.'

THE MOUNT

There was a wood. Before young rooks were flown
night cracked with their companionable cries,
trees leaned towards our beds. It was a house
we loved and kept a while, but could not own.

To there, one day, a boy came back from sea,
the Merchant Navy. He had lived, till eight,
in the old servants'-quarters. Between girls
and ships, he walked, then stood outside its gate.

He smoked. He wished, he said, to see the place.
The beeches breathed. I could not let him in.
We, too, had moved. I came back studying,
school, my excuse. I eyed his handsome face.

I think he gazed, then turned, and walked away.
I ran up the rough drive so I could see
if unseen mice had left more nibbled stones
in the dry darkness of the hollow tree.

What would I do now, if I, too, went back,
then stood before a child's anxious face?
I know the yews were taken from that place,
berries like glossy mouths, leaves' bitter black.

I would dig up those painted tiles we found
in ruined cottages, hid secretly
their tawny quince, split ruby pomegranates,
strange fruits a boy might carry home from sea.

MEMOIR

My mother cycled to the base
to teach. In the ploughed fields' place
green bunkers rose, a dead man's face.

'They had the rocket up today',
my mother said, in the bright way
of her own pupils. She could buy

the NAAFI's doughnuts, shower our plates
with juicy sugar, walls of sweet
white ash. She never lost the weight.

Our kitchen dreamed American dreams,
forgot its mangle. From a van
came second-hand twin-tub's rattling gleam.

But you, inside the wired gates
where the Alsatians leapt at bay,
camp guard's son, counted higher stakes.

We listened to the washer's purr.
Kerouac passed you in a blur
from your friends' kitchens. It was Thor,

the missile made with nuclear tip
which towered above the limestone's lip
until Kruschev turned back his ships.

Your email tears my world apart.
Sleepless, I count my launching heart.
Three, two, one, zero. Now I start.

A pocket of time was lent.
We left home. Country style,
I ached to drive a hundred miles
while you had flown a continent.

Taut greyhounds, we worshipped the mind,
let it burn through heart and bone.
But the body is all we own.
We wasted so much time.

The sourer plotters said of you,
fresh from apartheid's wire and cards,
you thought no English rule was hard.
Invisible gates close too.

Let me swim through the senses' pool!
My beads from Africa, from you,
burned kingfisher, raw orange, blue.
You wore soft socks, kind navy wool.

You found, from river's fogs and chill,
your aunt's warm house in Wales.
In your voice, her songs sailed
over the settlers' gravel.

Your tastes seemed plain: much tea,
thick, discreet biscuits. But fruit
perfumed my mouth, lovers' loot.
Then fathers raged. No heart slips free.

What did we do, later? Kind air
warmed. Wars flared. We vote
to shorten them. Words swill my throat.
You are the new Queen of the Air.

As I list each gain, loss and lack,
I have left one sense behind.
Remember a day of dark wind?
You opened my door, then reeled back.

Wired jasmine was wreathing the room,
its white breath your childhood heat.
It died; you moved on. No defeat.
Scent spills from time's pocket, our home.

IN THE SPARE ROOM

It was the nineteen-fifties, when we kept
soft string in coils, brown paper in small shrines,
when winter coats were passed down several times.
Foil milk tops had their own box in that house
for guide dog puppies, schools for Africa.
There, rustling in their river, came a mouse.

Then Mrs Haywood scrubbed floors for my mother
while she taught children at the US base,
glimpsed heaps of doughnuts, fridges' silver doors.
Mrs Haywood walked shyly to our house.
A child with a cleft lip, she had been teased.
She stared with kind distress upon the mouse.

I caught it in her blue-striped handkerchief:
the first of many, slowworms, moles, fat, lean.
Who now boils cloth, so all our sins wash clean?
We feasted, flew. We melted the far ice.
Mrs Haywood, quiet village soul, is dead.
Now, rustling through the world, I hear the mice.

WHAT?

It was a bus. It was the war.
It backed into the Brayford Pool
whose swans drifted towards the edge
like sparrows to a window ledge,
black at the heart of Lincoln. Or,
you have the story wrong, you fool,

it simply was your parents' fear
of what might happen, without lights.
Whether you skirt the reservoir
or eye the Severn's mud-slicked shore,
if, for one breath, you veer too near,
the wheels will swerve into the night.

It was the mailcoach, red as fox.
The panicked horses would not halt.
It was the wagon's freshest team
gone, overloaded, down the stream.
It was the cart with the best ox.
It was the bloody Romans' fault.

ARRANGED

What is in the jug? A shoot of holly
shockingly green, though drought now stunts the tree.
Roses of the pink of a thumbnail
where good blood quietly throbs. Geraniums,
crumpled, brilliant, soaring out of water,
all sprigs which I have sliced off by mistake
in careless gardening. Now they thrive for days,
which, left in noon's heat, would not last an hour,
things done in error, the odd corners
of our lives, which flower and flower.

PENSIONED

Yes, I saw Hezekiah Brown,
a tall man, stately, with one eye.
The shrapnel took it in the war,
the Great War. But he fought on, by
my grandfather, a gamekeeper
who would have shot him for a hare.

Fifty years on, he drove along
our village edge, his skewbald mare
hauling small scrap on a loose rein.
They stopped ten yards from the front door,
by wind-blown fuchsias, raspberries.
How had he learnt that Frank lived there?

And when he first drove to the sea,
my father gestured to a place
a green shelf by a small quarry,
quiet no man's land, sufficient space,
caravan, horse. Here Hezekiah
drove back to wife, high fires, then snored

like my grandfather, safe beneath
his Council roof. Fifty years more
we may own mortgages, a car,
send others' sons to distant war,
swim heated seas, keep no room for
a van, a horse, now we are poor.

IN MAY

The Cox's apple tree has blowsy swags,
a girl's bare shoulders, falling from a dress.
Hawthorn, though held bad luck, shines pale and neat,
a distant housewife, waving off her guest.
Untrimmed and unplanted, worn by weather,
one small tree's flowers burn red, unperplexed,
flash snow. Crab apples, in pale yellow pools
like sun, feed all, spilt, patient, wait the next.

CROPS

The roses are in season and
the sweetest is the German rose
whose name I think means happiness,
whose snow breathes June to lips and nose.
July booms in with thunderstorms.
Ask, in their growl, what ageing means:
stiff knees, lost names, a sudden wish
to turn from roses to broad beans.

For broad beans are in season and
my mother skinned them, then would cook
her fat white sauce, still sprinkled thick
with parsley. This my great-aunt took
to munch from rows, threw torn, raw green
into her morning porridge bowl.
She lived past ninety, grew broad beans.

I think they deserve their skins.
I think they do not need a sauce,
I chew on their glistening curves
as patiently as my old horse.
The pea's white flower, on crossed sticks, leans;
for months, potatoes plump. How short
is the warm season for broad beans.

THE METHODISTS

I knew the girls on climbing frames
who sang like cagebirds all break long
their Chapel anniversary song.

Its patterned bricks had birthdays too
with gales of singing, tea and treats.
The Chapel choir had doled-out sweets

to the contempt of us in Church,
quavering, glazed, in cheerless pews.
But England's gods stayed upper-class

despite the wild notes one girl dropped.
The Methodists told her not to sing
old, wicked songs. And so she stopped.

But at their fête in fitful sun
I heard their farmhand preacher, plain
in suit, thank God, then pray for rain.

Their Chapel closed, became a house.
Our Sunday morning worships cars.
The Methodists hated gambling, bars,

Bishops who prop up Royalty.
A glum Prince, his thin girl, will rule
whose Chapel guards a private school.

Now in my waste land, freedom, I
can sing the wild black songs again.
For the fourth week, we have no rain.

AMY

It was her voice that stopped you in your tracks
which made you drop the kitchen knife,
set down the vitamins, forget the cat,
which rocked you on the heels of your own life.
Bed, heart, skin spun. But you must pick
the shopping up, lock doors. She never did.
The vodka spilt. The knife cut to the bone.
The black CD waits in its box. She slurred.
The police will tell us if she died alone.

WRITING RINALDO

'Yes, Mr Hill. An opera in two weeks.'
He is twenty. The librettists hate the haste.
He chops cantatas, scours Venetian scores.
How Handel would have worshipped cut and paste.

Yet it is there, as water trickles through
small fingers in the troughs of a great sea.
Sorrow for all he lost, or never found.
The piled-up plates. The icy bed, still empty.

No, you must live with these, the music says,
although the groves of wandering flutes give joy
to girls, the passing 'prentice and the Prince.
Work! Leave your money to the coachman's boy.

'Yes, Mr Hill. I scored for fireworks.'
Lit faces cheer, although his critics rage
at painted waves. They mourn – as I do, too –
that promised horses never reached the stage.

Magician! Living sparrows twitter trees.
Castrati warble. No, I do not know.
His trumpets flare. The Saracens take flight.
The Siren rises from the undertow.

Already a young whale in music's sea,
he will return, with his own company,

huge dinners. His accounts are never wrong.
Breathless, he hums the slim girl's misery.
Lashed to himself, he scrawls the Siren's song.

SHANTIES

So these were chanted on slave-ships.
Why did I not guess before?
Because I hide from just men's rage,
can whistle softly, flick the page,
Shenandoah, O Shenandoah.

We count our own. Though tears fall hot,
we do not go back for more.
Out of the dust, let small ghosts come
as quiet as spent uranium,
Shenandoah, good Shenandoah.

'I love your daughter', sang the men,
hands on rope, some rough, some raw.
The colours arched above the rain,
they never sang so true again.
Shenandoah, O Shenandoah.

STRATA

The first geological map of Britain was made by William Smith in 1815.

Layer One

I, 'Strata Smith', first mapped out Stow,
the blacksmith's solid, brooding son.
Taught young to measure and survey
I tramped high ground, land strewn with stones,
flicked earth from coiled fossils, fingered
the frailest ferns of old, warm seas.
Before the ploughboy's cracked boots trod,
I labelled, boxed, gazed long at these.

I saw how shells slept, laid in layers,
limestone, 'Great Oolyte', chalk and coal.
They could be mapped. They could be mined.
On foot, on carts, I sensed my stones,
world under wold, the lime's blue veins,
hard bones beneath my own tanned skin.
I planned the West's canals, was sacked.
I could not keep the waters in.

Despite broad vowels, I struck good work,
our bedrock. I drained Prisley Bog,
fen to wide fields, wetland to plough.
His Grace shook my hand in chill fog.
Leaf deep on leaf, ink sketches piled
in lodgings. Pages' overlap
showed London clays of Shooter's Hill,
downs seas once overran, my map.

How could we fail? Grand, rival maps –
I called up counties. Gloucestershire's
fossils formed small, high Cuberley.
I pressed Dean's coal-black thumbprint clear.
'William Smith, Mineral Surveyor',
the title ran, my rich seam. If
idle eyes strayed, I washed, pale blue,
brown Avon's 'high, romantic cliffs'.

Pebble-kicked down those cliffs, I fell
to debtor's cells; once free, fled North,
mapped 'sections', London, Anglesey,
through mountains, Thames' mud, 'dipping South'.
Young scientists asked me to speak,
I mined old notes, walked to a friend,
strong, seventy. Rain chilled my bones.
Water will find us in the end.

Layer Two

I lick my moisture off the stones
of York Asylum. I was wife
to William, whom I do not blame,
a dark shaft sunk beneath his life,

mad Mary Ann, flawed specimen
aged sixteen to his forty, map
across our bed. I was the stone
that shatters to the hammer's tap.

Can your maps find my crumbled mind?
Do miners do the Devil's work?
But how I miss my fire! Would you
sit like a stone, spin Earth's own dark?

I scramble strata. What is 'fracking'?
Cheap gas, trucks for the farmer's lad,
the shaken homes of Oklahoma,
water made waste? You must be mad.

And do you know he sold the shells,
box piled on box? They passed me by,
I stayed my shout. His eyes shone wet.
I did not know a stone could cry.

But now I say what he could not.
His coloured maps were beautiful,
green chalks, gold crooked limestone's spine
from Severn to sea, which sweeps us all.

He traced fine bones beneath my skin.
He did not heat my sea or hill.
A quiet man field-walks Coberley,
updates screens with his colours, still.

Layer Three

There was a hot hillside at Stow,
a limestone fault, trickle of spring.
They rarely drain in Gloucestershire.
A thrush came, to bash shells, then sing.

How many plants grew in that bog?
My best work? No. I understand
geologists will not form a Royal
Society. I drop his hand.

I stare into my strata map,
eyes' green, her shoulder blade's gold tone.
I sit, without her, till I hear
clean water pulse the thrush's stone.

AFTERMATH

I cleaned two homes. I learned one thing.
What will survive of us is not
our careful words, our gardens' grace,
but rubber bands; green balls of string.

MONUMENT

Imperial London. The bronze horses rear
in autumn's sunlight on the highest ledge,
the driver wreathed. Peace? Triumph? But I see
the hoof-tips slip, unsteady, past the edge.

5:30 A.M.

As the lake's skin split I saw the monsters.
The main, the massive pair cruised side by side.
We had known of them. But not the others
like busy boats who crossed their wake. What were

the lorries doing, crawling our wet roads
in procession? Some were painted white,
blank as wedding cakes. But who was driving?
For one by one they vanished in the lake.

When first the huge drops fell, I turned to watch
the lighted cabins. There they ate and slept,
the girls who groomed the priceless frail racehorses,
the dancers who tied shoes as fine as skin.

Should I leave them to their frills and brushes
or cry to them of storms? Was I too late?
As I blinked on the landing, tired, uncertain,
I heard the lorry purring by the gate,
I saw the lorry waiting by my gate.

FALLING DOWN, FALLING DOWN

If I ate no cake,
if I ate two cakes,
if I lingered by biscuits,
disdained cauliflower,
if I had not turned
my face to the sun
if the man had not rushed
from the petrol station
dodging before me,
like you, a dancer,
if I had glanced down-

Is that my blood?
Are those my glasses?
That tooth will cost –
Thank you. Oh no!
Not an ambulance.
And don't call my husband.
I am used to this.
I have fallen off horses.
New raw, rich blood
drops warmly through tissue.
I will call A & E,
I promise. I lie.

'You've done it this time',
says the bathroom mirror.
My lip is two rags.
With the stained flannel clasped,
I set the cool yogurt,
the crisp and cruel celery
safe on their shelves.
Then I call upstairs.

If I shut my eyes
in Gloucestershire Royal
at one a.m.
I can tick them off,
the London trip,
the din of the party,
falling, falling. Here instead
is a girl in a wheelchair,
slightly less battered
than my changed face.
Her escort swears,
black-eyed, black-coated,
at stern Reception:
'They want me sectioned.'
They may be right.

Falling, falling
at Gloucestershire Royal
a fair-faced girl
pulls the threads tight,
white skin, rose flesh,
like plaits on a pony,
my black blood clotted,
thicker than night.
'How many stitches?'
'Ten', she shimmers.
Put back the cake.
Walk out, upright.

1642

Retired, I could research
our English Civil War.
Would digging pile dry earth
on all I knew before?
One street still holds a fair,
where it fought off a King.
Rocked in Cirencester

by siege-guns, weeks of noise,
quiet Lady X went mad,
unearthed her childhood toys,
lined dolls up till she died.
Faeries were frightened out.
In summer grass, men fell
who asked for honest votes.

Welcome, the smiling King!
Less welcome, the spy state,
spaniels and secret police,
the whispers at the gate.
Research the Civil War?
Let heavy books be dropped
back in the archive, for
this war has never stopped.

BREAKING THE FAST

When I am alone, toast is ceremony.
I cut bread thick (cooking is art),
discover butter for my cracked skin.
Toast must be hot, butter is chill.
I slide both in the microwave's loud glow,
wait for the chime, heap strawberries.
But I must eat it where I am,
perfect, alone. Love's toast is burned,
brought cold upstairs with the wrong jam.

THE 8:10 TO EDINBURGH

I listen in the cool cave, our back room,
it is eight-twelve. I hear the soft breath come
slide sun-baked sidings, meet our cutting's gloom,
check, echo, cough. This should have been my train.

I ride my own chair, bolt upright. How fast
the engine shrieks, first coaches squeal, the last
bolts like a pony, hammered, lost, the past,
the beast of power, the Scots express, my train.

I see red Midland breweries, hills break
to Lakeland skies. I see Scots castles ache
floodlit to dusk. Then town rooms, party, cake,
talk unheard, friends unseen, the darkened train.

The reason I am here lies on a bed,
a sleeping woman, tubes across her head,
ticket on wrist, scheduled to meet the dead,
travelling direct. I am not on that train.

FRIDAY AFTERNOON

It was the autumn's last day, when the roof
was skimmed by wings – Red Admiral butterfly? –
a glance of black against the sky, like truth.

It was the day on which the goldfinch flung
its yellow wing against the glass, as though
it had drunk all the sweetness from the sun,

by which, in the wild garden, hips were seen
swelled by the last night's rain, crowns under leaves,
as though they could stay glossy, ever green,

a day when children played and did not fall
when traffic slowed to world's edge, a gold crawl,
which I heard, sun-lapped, sleeping through it all.

SPECIES

Sometimes they rise before me in the night:
the lemurs, eyes as bare and bright as moons;
the lizard, ancient as the afternoon;
the coral's tender hands which sun bleached white.
Some are immense: the tiger, shot and still;
some thumbnail-sized, like Chile's emerald frog
I never saw, and soon, nobody will.

UNDER THE STAIRS

When it leapt from the cat, it found
its way into the cupboard's cool.

It made a nest of chewed-up wool
from an old sheepskin. Water lay

in the cat's dish, for night trips. Day
found it still warm but starving, curled

tuned into each slow step. Hot world
spun, dazed the garden, while it grew

weak as a kitten. The cat knew
its scent, striped angel, barred the door.

Did it die there, blunt nose on paws?
Or did I shift saddles, rug, balls,

to scoop it, trembling, past the hall,
to tides of seeds, which silt the shed?
Did it then blunder? Is it dead
or freed, to honeysuckle's night?

Stare at your door. A line of light.

Though I read 'Notes on Stars',
yet I always forget
the planet, or comet,
until my blank noon.
But our milkman saved me.
I saw on the dawn's step
the milk, then high Venus,
by her crescent moon.

They were a white iris,
as crisp as an eyelash,
a slim curve, a great blaze,
taut blue that too soon
is cars, is dulled daylight.
Look quick, you may catch them,
old Venus, though faded,
her smudged crescent moon.

POPPY SEEDS

Yes, they go everywhere, like breath.
They lodge in nails. They sweeten teeth,

strange food to me. Are they that haze,
red banks, once corn's, now motorways

or from some special flowers? I read
our newborn brain knows what we see

but not the words. They must be learned,
skilfully as these seeds were burned.

Oh, but I knew this. Before school
I spoke birds' nests, the blackbird's cool

mud, spoke eggs, the robin's scrawl.
I robbed no nest. The words took all.

Black seeds, the sweet sleep under grief,
give me the language of the leaf.

THE ELMS

We may know trees but rarely wood.
Elm was the workhorse, daily tree,
pale handle, for your fork and spade,
a chair as low as a bent knee
cut down for each uneven floor.
Women leaned into its curved back
as the milk pulsed, as birds once pressed
its crowded leaf, before storm's black.

The elms died fast, of one disease.
Is that a sapling, in the hedge?
No, hazel with its rose-flushed buds
then young lime with its heart-shaped edge.
Its step-grandchild must be the ash,
sprung on street corners, on stone hills,
until the lightning cracks the wind,
the crest is split, the fine twig spills.

But now ash has its own disease,
what can I still recall of elm?
Its seeds were white, softer than coins,
whose lack, or glut, would overwhelm.
On other paths, by other trees,
I stand, still in that storm of snow.
From park, low hedge, your elms still rise.
Look at them well, before they go.

LET

'Let the dead bury the dead!' he cried
far from shocked eyes of his mother.
But he had planed coffins, so knew
the dead belong to each other,
as wood fell, in pale silk curls,
which nested on shadowed boards there,
until his brush whispered it out,
to chickens, the yard and the air.

THE BRAMLEY

Only the English would breed such an apple,
so sour you must smother it with sugar.
I have had enough of all those women's pastry,
light as wheedling, blackmail in the butter,
their sugar hissed to hide all that is tart.

Give me Coxes. Give me Worcesters,
rosy, self-sweet. Let feet go shocked
back to the orchard grass, back to the start.

THE HORSE'S MOUTH

based on The Remnants of an Army, *Elizabeth Butler's paint-ing of one survivor of the massacre of sixteen thousand British soldiers and camp followers in the First Afghan War, 1842.*

Her blistered muzzle skims dry ground.
Tongue lolls past bit. Cracked hooves have found
the baked path to the fort.
The rider's leather palms grip round
his pommel. He has dropped the reins.
Scarlet sash swings, silk's battered skeins.
One red eye rolls, his dead pile plains.
One man, not caught.

The men who clatter through the gate
are also mounted, smart and straight.
The General's grey, in fear,
or puzzlement, lets fine head tilt.
The rider in the red skull cap,
rough Afghan sheepskin on his back,
does not part lips. Though his voice cracks
they will not hear.

To shaded rooms, on a tape's loop
a young voice from the present troop
speaks level, calm, on course:
'For me, it's Queen and Country!' Scoop
the sagging man. How, in such heat,
can Queen or country beat retreat?
Ask Generals. Ask recruits' torn feet.
Now ask the horse.

Plumed for the Household Cavalry
the young black bandsman, brass on knee,
told me he never learned to ride
before the Army. Bruised, astride
huge Irish hunters, he clung on –

So one small ploughboy, plumping for
the cavalry's ranks for his Great War,
who left the sucking clay of fields,
hay-loaded creak of wagon's wheels
found himself perched, sky-high, on Bess,
white, bony, older than the rest.
'Recruits', the bandsman told me, 'can't
pick and choose their favourite mount.'

The farm boy, his short legs like straw,
shivered in Egypt's sun, before
their first charge. How would she keep up?
The trumpets shook the sweating troop,
then, shot-wise, as a partridge runs,
Bess spun, then galloped from the guns.

EIGHT

He stayed in Crete. The family
beckoned him up, one day, to see
a small back room, a curtained niche.

A photograph? A daughter dead?
Or slubbed gold heaven, the icon's head?
Cloth dragged the boards with its rough swish.

They held their ground. They stood in rows,
unlaced, like prisoners', heels to toes,
eight pairs of paratroopers' boots.

One was bashed by an olive tree,
one scuffed by rock. How carefully
they had been eased from each warm foot.

One listener asked, 'Were they for spares?'
'No', he said firmly. They stood there
polished in ranks. It was a shrine.

The deaths that were. The deaths to come –
By sea's first sigh, the thyme-bees hum.
Eight pairs of boots march down the line.

CRITICISM

'Good Muses keep hands clean!'

'Do they?' she frowns,
sets down the stable fork,
picks up the baby,
welds in the wartime factory
until the siren wails,
notices, in silence,
the whiteness of my nails.

WILTON PARK (WHERE PHILIP SIDNEY WROTE ARCADIA)

Why have I never read *Arcadia*?
Because I sensed doors in the dark.
For William Herbert swept a village far
out of his green and perfect park
until the starving shepherds spilled
back to his lawn, were clubbed and killed.

THE NORTH

Bears had been known to lick his test gear, or
a cub would fell it, with one yellowed paw.
The boat each day found him a new ice mass.
Careful as child, he sank his first, small tracks,
filled up his sheet with figures. In the slack
of noon, sea nosed around its bergs. Too wide.
He counted hours, until his boat bobbed back.

He listed every name for stars of ice,
each quiet explosion, cracks spread to crevasse.
He monitored each gap. He felt no fear,
yet caught, like sailors once, a breath of flowers,
tapped in his journal, 'We should not be here.'

3:12 A.M.

No eye should see this golden, drunken moon,
setting on her back, an hour too soon.

2 A.M.

Then, when she woke,
she did not know if she was young.
But her coffee was cold
and everyone had gone.

STILL DARK

Three a.m. The water strokes your chin.
Now tell yourself – and firmly – you can swim.

FIRST

The light goes; leaves us darkly, all night through.
Then the light leaves, but takes us too.

HOME

I heard of her by radio.
She was the little girl of two
her mother left alone, to go
partying for a week with friends.
The neighbours heard her crying, so
the mother's jailed. The story ends.

The cold wet clothes. The empty wall –
appalled, the mind goes tumbling back –
the sobbing rush into the hall.
Her mother claimed she did go back,
reheated food, four times in all,
then off into the spinning black.

Briefly, I am that child, as she
who felt locks bite, will always be.
Briefly, though sober, only for
a heart's skip, I, too, slammed that door.

'WILL THE COMET SURVIVE ITS ENCOUNTER WITH THE SUN?'

(astronomer, writing of Comet Ison)

This, I suppose, is what we do,
we fly into the sun
and some are gone and some survive
like shadows, limping on.
And some, far closer than the stars,
fill all our eyes at dawn.

EX-TUTOR (1937–2014)

What should I list? Her agile mind,
husband and sons she left behind,
jobs she secured, terms she refined?
March wind is bitter. She was kind.

It began, like wonder, back there
in the village's dark huddle
which I can never visit, like a star.

In high orbit, warm muddle,
my father's hard-packed arms, I passed.
Winter wind stilled, hedge and puddle

pure ice. Above my wreath of breath,
the weak eye of the one streetlight
beyond Back Lane and Temple Garth,

skies pricked with white until the night
swam with its stars. In their grave blaze
they filled my gaze like wings in flight

which never left, unlike the house,
the anxious moves, my mother's care.
For years I stood by my own house

with books and charts. My father there
could only name the tilted Plough
he followed with the snorting pair.

But I found Pegasus, the slow
sweep of the Swan, a fierce red eye,
the Bull. I watched the Hunter go

with frost's belt, over towns where I
now lived, where, still, the galaxy
boiled by his sword in clouding sky.

The books are laid aside. I see
new roofs, more weak lamps. Whirled and free
the stars, my calm dead, walk with me.

FALSE THAW

The wind begins to rise. The migrant birds
who have haunted the trees for days with their hiccuping cries,
who pecked the frozen apples to red pulp,
who thronged our ground to bicker, gobble, gulp,
have gone. Now past the widening ring of stains
late walkers totter ice, without a sun,
sense a moist breath, the great Atlantic's, come,
then slide where frost grips; with the birds, fall dumb.

NOVEMBER BEGAN

And the fieldfares blew
over the hedgetops, like grey leaves.

AFTER THE ALARM, CHRISTMAS DAY

I am up at five-ten. My daughter cooks.
I come down to scurry, brush mud from floors,
bear, from the garage, a great mast of sprouts,
find lemons, spice, all that she needs.
At the windows' height a band of rich light
licks royal blue, the young moon's dress,
hangs pale, the old moon's beads.

CHRISTMAS ON THE RADIO

With breakfast come ironic song selections,
one crooner who has Mafia connections,
a grey singer who longs for a white Christmas.
The station with the weather drowns in carols,
sung with a local and lugubrious gloom
from merrily on high. Outside this room

in the damp yard, I brush unending dark,
one thin trickle of birds' song, not the lark.
Robin, in ivy, starlings, in town roofs,
wet half-forgotten corners are the proof
these maddening, ever-burnished tunes ring right.
Now the sun sleeps. We wake to our own light.

There is a low glare in the sky
sweeps to a rainy night.
The planet's wrong, the house unsold,
and, after thirty years, you write.

My cycle coat blows on the line.
The old cat paws the door.
I tell you I am badger grey,
but wiser than before.

I do not tell you that I cried
since it was not for you
but for a child, since they break hearts
as no mere man can do.

But now my child is married,
the ones who fought me, dead,
and I am moved by your hands' grace
beside my clumsy head

although I cannot see you
and will not again.
My yellow coat flies like a flag.
The long night turns to rain.

FOR THE NEW YEAR

She was delighted by the sudden gift
after thirty years. How old must he be?
She had seen one shot, the skin still beautiful,
while her face carried the sorrows of the world
below her eyes. No, better not to meet,
reply discreetly. Why had he sent it now?
Safety in numbers? Flutters in the heart?
It was good (she told herself) not to be young,
not to bear that unending sadness, hope.
The sun was frowning before massive storms.
She stowed the gift. She kept the envelope.

First, as I peer, I hear the scrape
where the sharp stone's edge cut to bone
beneath the hair, the skin, the fat.
Next, deer or bison come

with fragile legs and capes of fur
scratched, like the shadow's dancing line,
tossed heads, recalled by stiffening hands,
while the last oil burned down.

Why did the spotted horses run?
Who were the men with wolves for heads?
Quick dream, before half-frozen beds?

I do not think they shaped stone gods,
or carved for hours to ward off harm.
The East wind blows down Oxford Street.
They made these things to keep them warm.

AFTER CATULLUS

I hate. I love. 'How can this be—?' you start.
I do not know. But I am torn apart.

NEXT

We read their lives, we know they will head for
the Asylum, or the War,
the one Great Love. But who can show
where we are stumbling, whistling—? Oh.

THE IRISH BUSKER

for Michael Donaghy, who played by ear

The silver tube sings at her lips.
There is no note more pure,
more strange. But darkness slips
down my warm clothes, my carriers' loot,

for this is death, for now, no spring,
no pulse of star, wind's blustering,
will echo back your battered flute.

FOR ANNA ADAMS

1926–2011

Some remember your strict verse,
some, your painting's other half.
I remember you said, 'Never
get between a cow and calf'.

AFTER READING THE COLLECTED POEMS OF VERONICA FORREST-THOMSON (1947–75)

Would she want couplets, long or quick?
Her hair combed to the cleanest flick
she brushed down words, the fine, the plain.
She knew that beauty needs a brain,
wore green rings, could measure season,
clung to rhyme, as if to reason.

Translated, theory never fits.
The sharp mind cuts itself to bits.
Greyed, I guess we cannot know
at first; must dress in trust, then go.
Did grief or squalor claim her young?
Most honourably, her friends stay dumb.

Her own words wait: her best defence.
She fought for love with ruined sense.
Bought flowers fell. The songs' rush slowed,
deep in their steel, the fuel rods glowed
with a design, now thought unsound,
whose coolant circled, round and round.

Then the salt water swept inland
turned homes to kindling, roads to sand.
Technicians don their page-white clothes,
know minutes mount a fatal dose.
Then, in the ticking quiet she heard,
they hack and save, without a word.

DICKENS: A DAYDREAM

The scrapman's son bangs at our door,
skives school, like father, grandfather,
all crammed in van's hum. 'Anything, sir?'
curls wild, your scavenging people.

The doe-eyed girl at the café till
is child's height, yet does not spill
one bean from heaped trays, hammers bills,
your frantic, stunted people.

Bad teeth, bent hips, the pitbull's snarl
called you out from the lawyer's yarns.
Happiness bored you most of all,
white tables, good, quiet people.

One was your wife. You glimpsed ahead
the young actress's breasts instead,
buds crushed by silk. She never said
your name, changed dates, fooled people.

London, in its lost party time,
the trees' lit snow, the towers' gold chime,
the heat of bars, the twist of lime,
you shun as in a fever.

We meet beneath the dripping bridge,
soot, fear and sorrow on each ledge.
Hurt child, you scour each rag-strewn beach,
walk all night, stride and shiver

until the dawn strikes London's walls
and clangs Good morning from St Paul's.
Waitresses, Poles, striped bankers pour,
your million words. Sleep, river.

AFTER MEETING A FRIEND OF SYLVIA PLATH

She would have been as old as you.
She might have freckles on her hands,
a stick, one knee which would not bend.

Would she read slowly through her book,
not flick, so quickly, to the end?

Three Poems from Steep (page 24)

(I) Letter, 1917: 'Baba' was Edward and Helen Thomas' youngest child, Myfanwy (with whom I corresponded when she was ninety-four). The poem's last two lines are taken from a letter written by Edward to Helen on 17 March 1917. He was killed on 9 April 1917.

(II) No 2, Yewtree Cottages: This is the last home of Edward Thomas in Steep, Hampshire. It is now in private hands. I visited the garden, by kind permission of its owner, during the making of a BBC radio programme.

Writing Rinaldo (page 39)

Aaron Hill was the dynamic young manager of the Theatre Royal, Drury Lane, who staged the first performance of 'Rinaldo'.

Strata (page 41)

Layer One: In 1806, Smith described his draining of Prisley Bog, one of his 'extraordinary improvements' for the Duke of Bedford and other landowners.

Layer Two: 'In 2009 there were 50 quakes in Oklahoma. In 2010 there were more than 1,000' (*The Independent*, 7/4/14). Cuberley (now Coberley) is a small Gloucestershire village. In its fields I have met William Smith's heir, a man from the Geological Survey.

Layer Three: Because of the Republican leanings of some of its early Fellows, the Geological Society of London refused to be called 'Royal'.

Skies (page 70)

'Temple' refers to the Knight Templars, who once controlled part of the village's land. 'Garth', a Viking word, is used here of a farmyard.

ACKNOWLEDGEMENTS

Grateful acknowledgement is made to the editors, presenters and producers of the following publications and broadcasts in which some of these poems were first published:

A Mutual Friend: Poems for Charles Dickens (ed. Peter Robinson, Two Rivers, 2012); *Accompanied Voices* (ed. John Greening, Boydell, 2015); *Acumen*; *Agenda*; *andotherpoems*; *Angle*; *The Apple Anthology* (ed. Yvonne Reddick & George Ttouli, Nine Arches Press, 2013); *ARTEMISpoetry*; *Bards in the Bog* poster (Shetland Public Libraries); BBC Radio Gloucestershire Breakfast Show (presented by Mark Cummings); *Blackbox Manifold*; *The Book of Love and Loss* (ed. R. V. Bailey & June Hall, Belgrave Press, 2014); *The Countryman*; *Crystal Voices: Crystal Clear Creators* (ed. Maria Taylor, 2015); *The Emma Press Anthology of Age* (ed. Sarah Hesketh); *For Rhino in a Shrinking World* (ed. Harry Owen, The Poets Printery, 2013); *Front Row* (BBC Radio 4, produced by Julian May); *Sunday Folk* (BBC Radio Shropshire, presented by Genevieve Tudor); *The Guardian*; *Hallelujah for 50 ft Women* (ed. Raving Beauties, Bloodaxe, 2015); *Handel News*; *Heart Shoots* (ed. Ronnie Goodyer, Indigo Dreams, 2013); *Ink, Sweat and Tears*; *The Interpreter's House*; *Kin Journal*; *The Lake*; *The London Magazine*; *Magma*; *Map* (ed. Michael McKimm, Worple, 2015); *New Walk*; *The North*; *PN Review*; *Poetry in the Waiting Room*; *Poetry London*; *The Poetry of Sex* (ed. Sophie Hannah, Penguin, 2014); *Poetry Wales*; *The Price of Gold* (ed. Joy Howard, Grey Hen, 2012); *Proletarian Poetry*; *Proms Plus* (BBC Radio 3, 2011); *The Reader*; *The Rialto*; *Slow Things* (ed. Rachel Piercey & Emma Wright, The Emma Press, 2015); *Scintilla*; *Snakeskin*; *Something Happens, Sometimes Here* (ed. Rory Waterman, Five Leaves, 2015); *Stand*; *The SHOp*; *The Spectator*; *The Stare's Nest*; *Times Literary Supplement*; *Transitions* (ed. Joy Howard, Grey Hen, 2015); *Zambia Grade 11 English Learner's Book* (ed. Hurbert Kakonkanya et al, Oxford University Press, 2015).